Also by Carolyn Smart:

The Way to Come Home
At the End of the Day, a Memoir
Stoning the Moon
Power Sources
Swimmers in Oblivion

HOOKED

seven poems

Carolyn Smart

Brick Books

Library and Archives Canada Cataloguing in Publication

Smart, Carolyn
    Hooked : seven poems / Carolyn Smart.

Poems.
ISBN 978-1-894078-69-6

1. Women--Poetry. I. Title.

PS8587.M37H66 2009   C811'.54   C2008-906881-5

We acknowledge the Canada Council for the Arts, the
Government of Canada through the Book Publishing Industry
Development Program (BPIDP), and the Ontario Arts Council
for their support of our publishing program.

The cover painting is a detail from *Interior/Exterior Zanzibar
Tea Gardens*, 1986, mixed media on paper, 30" x 67",
© Sarindar Dhaliwal.

The author photograph was taken by Bernard Clark.

The book is set in Sabon and AG Buch Condensed.

Design and layout by Alan Siu.

Printed and bound by Sunville Printco Inc.

Brick Books
431 Boler Road, Box 20081
London, Ontario N6K 4G6

www.brickbooks.ca

For Georgette Fry

Was it not ourselves who frightened us most?
As if brightness or sweetness could save us.

— Lavinia Greenlaw, *"Zombies"*

Why has the will an influence over the tongue and fingers, not over the heart or liver?

— David Hume

Contents

Written on the Flesh

Myra Hindley: July 23, 1942–November 15, 2002

> Mass murder is a novel written on the flesh
> — Ian Brady: 1938–

I

this is what it was:
Ian's hands

he could make me laugh
and what else?

that first night he took me to the pictures:
all those people at Nuremberg, cheering,
better than a football match

his nails were clean
and he read books

we met at Christmastime,
an office party at Millwards

II

as a girl I
used to write a lot of stories
laughed and sang
made up jokes
was bad at needlework
couldn't bear domestic science

loved the mouth organ
played it for Maureen
mums liked me
I was a good babysitter

was a Catholic, took communion
after that boy drowned I cried
and prayed and prayed

God is a disease, a plague, a weight round a man's neck
said de Sade
oh, God, yes
said David, who was there,
while his wife Maureen sat home with Mum

what's all the noise about
Gran asked
it's just the dogs I said

III

the books we read:
The Pleasures of the Torture Chamber
Kiss of the Whip
Heinrich Himmler
The Anti-Sex
De Sade

on the weekends we'd picnic
take the dog
take the pictures
Ian would write it up

Cradle of Erotica
Sexual Anomalies and Perversions
The Mark of the Swastika

we studied German
Ian looks a bit like Goebbels,
people said that

didn't know you could buy those kinds of books
saw them down the shops in Manchester
could walk right in
and there they'd be, so easy

IV

I was good, worked hard
shorthand, typing
dressed well, pulling up my stockings
with my long white hands

see this one
taken in the garden?
I like the black and whites

made my hair peroxide blonde
only proper, like Irma Grese
I'd look at her picture and think about her
schnell, she said, *hurry*, laughing at her hangman,
at Bergen-Belsen she'd stand there
in her hard boots, cellophane whip
she ate up every minute of it
the sound her dogs made when she let them at it
I can see that in her face
pure joy

V

we talked so much
we made it happen:

Pauline
was July
she was 16
I was 21

Ian and I lived with Gran
we'd go to work come home have tea
listen to the tapes

see this one of me with the dog?
I'm looking down at John 12 dead and buried underground
then Keith 12
then Lesley Anne 10

no I didn't have anything to do with it
I stood at the window
and he killed her
though he said I did it

with my bare hands
her screaming in her socks and shoes
Please, Mummy, please!

we played Ray Conniff's "Little Drummer Boy"

it made the jury weep
to hear it
(Ian was busy with the mints)
wherever he has been, I have been too

VI

at my funeral I want Mum, my nephew,
and I want David
he's seen things

stood in the sitting room
and thought Ian danced with a rag doll

there was blood on my shoes
I stood at the window
Gran said *what's all the noise about*

she slept on the floor elsewhere that night
because we didn't want her there
asking stupid questions

14 blows to the head
with the fireplace axe

you fucking dirty bastard Ian said
god it was a mess, brain porridge, bone bits
and the blood
god it was everywhere
we laughed:
the look on his face!

and David barfed
he couldn't sleep he puked so hard
Maureen said call the coppers
they went down the call box

little git
Maureen married a boy

VII

when Maureen was born
I went to live with Gran
a back-to-back it was
smelled like grease
the ticking on and off
of electric fires
dust
stupid radio all day

Maureen lived with Mum
David was 15 and had his troubles
but she married him

what else was there to do?
by then it was Ian, me, Gran
Ian talked so much
David called it rubbish
sometimes he did

Maureen said she was afraid
no, not Ian,
it was David was the handful

she had a baby
after we were put away:
her stomach swelling up
putting on those little clothes
button nose and eyes like currants

VIII

they wrote about my voice
no-ah
that's how I spoke denial

what does Cambridge know of Crumpsall?

my harsh voice threatened, they wrote

snot running down the mouth of Lesley Anne
she shouldn't have been out that time of night
no-ah
no-ah
no but I said I was cruel

did the stylist in the remand
chat with me
as she combed out my stiff hair?

they said I used bad language
filthy niggers
dirty coloureds
yes-ah

I would talk that language
I could do all that

they had no bloody idea what I could do

IX

look at me here.
do I look like me?
this is me.
I have soft eyes

so many fell in love with me:
Janie Jones
Nina Wilde (*sharp mind and great wit*
that was me)
you know Longford did
Astor paid my way
I mean why else?

someone took me walking in Hyde Park
lovely, it was, the grass and everything
call her Jane Doe
and then there was Jane Doe
and Jane Doe

so they moved me from Holloway
Durham
Cookham Wood
Highpoint

and yet I managed a degree
Myra Hindley B.A. (Humanities)
thank you, Open University
thank you everyone

X

they only knew three at first:
John, Lesley Anne, Edward

but two more were done
Pauline, Keith

and let me tell you this
there was certainly one more:
Ann West

it was necessary that she hear it
16 minutes 21 seconds
that she say it:
yes the voice is that of
Lesley Anne, my child

ativan, temazepam, trizolam, quazepam
valium, meprobamate

her girl would come to her in dreams
she tried all kinds of hocus pocus
mediums, the lot

said if she had a chance
she'd kill me with her own bare hands

the cancer rotted out her liver first

XI

Marcus Harvey made a painting
the way they make those dots
look like a picnic by the sea

he made a painting of my Irma face
he made it out of handprints
of a child

I was 57 then
they threw things at the painting of my face
their loathing

look at me:
the raccoon eyes
porcelain face

I have a cruel, hard streak inside me

what do you think I dream?

XII

40 cigarettes a day,
my face so badly slashed
they used a team to fix me

now look at me:
heavy eyebrows
more than a hint of moustache
flat brown hair
you'd pass me in the street and never know

cerebral aneurysm,
depression,
osteoporosis

a good Catholic woman
my priest said
that made me laugh
and I spent hours in prayer

to talk of Ian
I am drenched in rage

XIII

heart attack
and the first crematorium wouldn't take me

in Cambridge Crematorium I lay
like radioactive waste with an afterlife

and they burned me
and they put me in the ground

became a better person after all

The Luckiest Girl in the World

Unity Valkyrie Mitford: August 8, 1914–May 28, 1948

I

the first time I saw him
my hand shook with such a violence
the tea spilled

he spoke so calmly in the Osteria, it was June
he sat with friends beneath the pergola:
still, it was, as if the world did not revolve around him

they said I'd always been a serious, awkward girl,
he made me beautiful

I sat at his feet and he stroked my hair:
never been so happy in my life

there is a bullet in the middle of my brain. *now*
please tell me who I am

conceived in Swastika, named Unity Valkyrie,
what else did they expect of me?

Farve read one book:
it was so good he never read another.
Muv had seven babies, only one a boy:
we girls were not allowed to go to school,
there was the library, Nanny Blor,
the governesses, we had no need for more

I loved Harrod's Zoo:
bought a snake, a rat, and a salamander there
Farve fetched a pony home in a taxi,
it was jolly good fun

when we were short of money
Muv gave up napkins,
we were not to let the food touch our lips,
the sound of tines against teeth at every meal
and me loading in the mashers and the chocs,
my teeth so brown and strange
they looked like Stonehenge

Muv raised chickens to pay for the governess
and Farve went prospecting in Swastika

From Batsford *Mansion* to Asthall *Manor* to
Swinbrook *House* to Old Mill *Cottage*
that's how it was with us Mitfords
we were debutantes

III

Decca and I had a language
she was my Boud, I was her Boud
she said I was *uuge and objegzionable*
we would argue to tears and then she'd shout
gommid id when she'd had enough

I really did my best,
I wanted so badly to die
there in the *Englischer Garten,*
in the calm afternoon of summer
on a bench at the end of the path

IV

Diana, most beautiful of sisters,
took me to the *Parteitag*.
She was in love with Oswald Mosley
and I was just nineteen,
there were hundreds of thousands at Nuremberg,
my body was electric
the *Führer's* splendour pouring through me
I was an angel in Bavaria

in the photographs before, I hid my teeth
nothing caught my attention until now

Muv was pleased:
a finishing school in Munich
such a good idea for her Bobo

I learned the language swiftly
because the *Führer* knew no English
I could do the salute everywhere
that arm clicking up to the sky like a warm machine
even my heels were eager,
my lipstick bright as flame

they said that Jews were being beaten
Jolly good, serves them right,
we should go and cheer, I said

V

I found out what he liked, where he ate
and I ate there too
at a table by myself, book in hand

Muv made me come home for a rest,
I shared a room with my Boud
her side littered with the *Daily Worker*,
mine had swastikas on the wall
and photos of the *Führer*, framed

Decca said she would hide a pistol in her pocket
just to shoot him dead

at the parties and balls I played yo-yo
and carried sweet Ratular on my neck
I talked about my friends,
how Julius Streicher brought the Jews up from the cellar
and had them eat grass
but darling, he was a kitten, Diana said,
such a sweetheart with his shining head
some kind of jewel

I think he loved me, Streicher
there were many likely men in Munich,
those darling Storms,
but I waited only for my *Führer*
would have done anything he asked

VI

February 9, 1935:
when he came in I saw him glance my way,
how many times had he seen me there,
cream cakes on the table,
my solemn eyes

Deutelmoser came and asked if I would care to join them
I walked over and the *Führer* stood up and saluted,
he shook my hand and introduced me to the others:
I sat there for more than half an hour
I don't remember all the things we spoke of:
I said he should come to England,
he said he'd love to but perhaps it was unwise,
there might be a revolution if he did

had I ever been to Bayreuth for the Wagners?
No I said, but I should like to,
he told his men to remember this next time

he knew London from his architecture studies,
loved *Cavalcade* best of all films,
said how good the roads were in Germany.
And then he signed a postcard: to Fraulein Unity Mitford
as a friendly memento of Germany
and Adolf Hitler

he paid my bill
and left
I am the luckiest girl in the world,
he is the greatest man of all time

VII

I'm a big blonde girl
with a big blonde body
and I want no one touching it

I like to wait
and when rewarded by a meeting
my heart rises up like a zeppelin,
all the banners waving and the anthems,
the crowds of lovely marching boys in step

I talked to him about difficult things
about how people still supported Jews
or how they didn't believe everything the *Führer* said
I worshipped him,
there was no one else.
I was never a nice girl
I made Party members disappear

I made them all frightened of my words
I talked and talked

VIII

140: that was the number of times I met with him
in all those busy years I don't know how he ever found the time

and his smile when he saw me,
his face would melt with tenderness, Diana saw it too:
you two here? he'd say, and he'd be happy

with him we went to the Olympics, to Bayreuth,
(his favourite was *Parsifal*)
we'd sit next to Eva, the looks she'd give me!
she didn't understand, it was never like *that*
between us.

we'd talk sweetly about pets and music
I didn't like it when he talked of cars
but there was much we had no need to discuss:
I made it crystal clear in my letter to *Der Stürmer*:
If you have room in your paper for my letter,
please publish my name in full...
I want everyone to know I am a Jew hater

Muv and Farve ordered me home for the summer
I had their full attention now

when I came back to Munich,
Muv met the *Führer*, of course she found him charming,
and Tom was content, saluting everywhere

IX

Decca was a Communist
Diana was a Fascist
Nancy was a volunteer
Debo had a wild time with young boys at the Ritz
Tom was a brownshirt
Pam opted out
Farve hated the beastly Hun
Muv thought them marvellous

and then there was Austria, Sudetenland, Poland,
those panzers rolling in and the beautiful Storms dying,
everyone was leaving
they begged me to go home
but I believed it would never come to blows,
our two great nations always meant to be together,
but on the 3rd of September the consulate called me round,
they handed me a telegram saying it was war

I no longer knew what happiness was.
I wrote a letter: *I send my best love to you all
and particularly to my Boud*
and I drove to the *Englischer Garten*
it was beautiful there and so green
I put my little silvered gun against my temple
and I pulled the trigger

Muv said I was the first casualty of the war

now I have a bullet in my brain
and a shattered heart

X

my *Führer* came to see me in the hospital
he brought flowers, said he'd pay all the bills,
that they were to care for me, care,
I put my Party badge deep in my mouth
and swallowed that golden possibility
I tried again and again
but nothing worked
and they sent me home on a train

I called the sugar chocolate, the salt I called tea
but we were so happy, the three of us,
just Muv, Farve, and me

XI

incontinent and clumsy
impatient and angry
I had no concentration,
I limped and staggered
I spilled and dropped my food.
Farve could not bear to see me eat,
he shouted at Muv and then
he just packed up his things and moved away

Muv hired a daily
to wash my sheets each morning
I biked around the village singing hymns
I became a Christian Scientist
loving God as sweetly as a child

reporters hated that I looked so well,
I went to Debo's wedding and my gloves were very clean
they couldn't see beneath my fringe:
the scar a sort of wormhole,
they said I should be put away
like Diana, like Mosley,
I was despised

everyone came to see me 'cept my Boud, my Decca,
she lived in America and they wanted to pay her money
but she never told a soul my story
I was her *huge, bright adversary* she said

XII

Decca had a baby who died,
Debo's baby was born dead,
Diana had four babies
Tom died in Burma
one of the last casualties of the war

I was all alone with Muv
and she was good to me,
never lost her temper once
though she missed Farve and I was
beastly
all the time

that old bullet started rumbling in 1948
when I looked up and said *I'm coming*
Muv's heart sank

I had a seizure
that night I died at last

no one had ever had such a happy young life
as I did up until the war

Rickety Rackety

Zelda Sayre Fitzgerald: July 24, 1900–March 10, 1948

I

moonlight

scent of January jasmine

my momma never spoke of the treachery of beauty
all the great sad stars once envied me the Alabama sky

sure as sugar I told tales and they were told of me
my redgold hair and famous mouth

Mon Capitain, I will make you:
swear the same

II

I loved the flow of water on my back
in the late afternoon when the glare was off the river
and the boys lay cool in the shade
their frank and naked eyes on mine
pear trees dropped their intemperate pulp

drowned in the lush of it I could simply explode
a honey bee battle, the trees themselves alive
and I adrift in grief for my tragic imaginary tribe
of Indians, lawless and unfettered

I danced the Shimmy and the Toddle,
raised my hemline to my knees
didn't drink or smoke
was bored and restless quicker than ordinary girls
once I stole a streetcar and drove it round the town
I was fire itself, a windstorm

III

my momma was a beauty with four daughters
my poppa a judge
and I the baby girl who drove him wild
why, he'd chase me round the supper table,
carving knife in hand

remember? you must have thought us lunatics
but loved me with a desperation anyway
didn't you, sweetheart?
they all did, fly boys buzzing the house
and a whole fraternity named for me

at eighteen I wanted to be gone, pure gone
and when I moved that way I drew a crowd

but once, up in the graveyard of the blessed Confederate dead,
I was just fifteen when Scott those boys

don't tell

IV

I was eighteen when we met
my hair flying my dance card full
you stood at the edge of the room and watched
my Seven Veils
though I didn't ask your name
you told me anyway

you were like heaven itself: your Princeton face
your guarantees of fame
my poppa asked if you were ever sober
I wasn't eager right away
I knew Montgomery and the Carolina hills
but the North was all you offered
and the pretty words you spoke

no notion what I might do next
you cracked your heart wide open
everybody did
but I saw you on my porch in the honeysuckle shade:
your confident eyes, uniform so white
your gin breath bitter on my mouth

I knew you, watched your agitation when
I first took off my clothes
laid my head on your irresolute chest
I always loved that place where your hair began
it was a blow that I was not pure
though I faked it pretty well

you said you'd never tell
you're just a liar

V

when you married me in New York
I was your blonde
your Viking
your madonna!
not even my friends were there
not my momma
I was a sweet belle no more
no southern more
no nothing
and I lay in my bed in the Biltmore Hotel
lost for the very first time

we were big drinkers, bad spellers, fast
spenders
we were spoiled children
like rattlesnakes we'd fight
I couldn't get enough of you

oh dearest, dearest, my lovely Goofo

I look down the tracks and see you coming
and out of every haze and mist
your darling rumpled trousers are hurrying to me

It's like begging for mercy of a storm
or killing Beauty or growing old, without you
lover, lover, Darling

VI

it was a rickety world
a rackety world of brow-beating the heart
we were feral those days
men left their hats all over town
spent hours putting interpretations on things
a wild burst of friends spent half an hour revolving
in the revolving door
Goofo wrote like an angel they said
and the money just plain flowed in and plain flowed out

baby was having a baby
and so we sailed for Europe:
me and Goofo in a gondola, Goofo at Fiesole
Paris was shabby, Spain disappointing, Algiers even worse
where was a place fine enough for our nativity?

we sailed for home

in Minnesota the moon and Indian forests
and the sleeping porch: I was heavy
and afraid of the thunder
while leaves blew up the streets
we waited for our child to be born
but when she came, dear god she was a beauty,
I said *Goofo I'm drunk, Mark Twain,*
isn't she smart, she has the hiccups, I hope it's
beautiful and a fool
a beautiful little fool
and you wrote it all down
you named her Scottie
as if she were yours alone

I miss the slow creak of the garden swing
the rusty croaking of the frogs in the cypress ponds

not allowed at Scottie's baptism
your parents thought I'd misbehave
I'm a fat girl lonely for my home

VII

exhausted by drink and debt
we went again to Paris where the 20th Century lived
everyone so young
and we loved our friends

we knew Picasso we knew Léger we knew Miro
we knew Joyce we knew Stein we knew Hemingway
we loved the Murphys and they loved us
and we moved to the South to be near them

Goofo wrote *Gatsby*, I let the sea exhaust me
we warmed our backs, invented cocktails
played in the sand
and once I turned my eyes sideways
couldn't help myself but stroke some creature there
we both told that tale so many times
when that boy read it, he would not know himself

I don't know now how far we went
beyond a kiss my dear

when the liquid dark came down
I'd grab the wheel and drive us to the edge
at Eden Roc I'd throw off my gown and dive

we don't believe in conservation

VIII

Say-ra Murphy admired Ernest Hemingway

but I guess he liked to look at me,
my *hawk's eyes, nigger legs,*

that's what he called them
Don't you think Al Jolson is greater than Jesus, I said
he called me crazy
and said Goofo was a rummy

whatcha know bout that, then, Say-ra?

I loved Scott Fitzgerald:
his jonquil hair
his saffron hands that smelled of cigarettes
and the sweat he wiped from his soft green palms,
his stomach rounded like a bowling ball
my darlin' Goofo's gone to pot at thirty-one

I sat and watched it all, chewed my lips
and wrung my hands
I smiled for no good reason
or was it just a rictus

IX

the night Scott grovelled at the feet of Isadora
I threw myself headlong down stone stairs

then we went to Africa and when we came back
he did not want me

I knew everyone in Paris talked about me every day
I saw phantoms and I tried to die

god help me what it is to be mad

I went to institutions:
Malmaison, Valmont, Prangins

I am a person—or was—of some capability
I do not want to lose my mind

X

the enemas the toxins the morphine break my skin:
eczema so extreme my head evaporates with pain
when they wrap me in fluid and mud
I want so much to flee

Goofo, what do you write these days
but a tale of my woe?
It was never good-hearted where we were
all I ask is that you keep my fractious secrets

oh Goofo though you won't see me
I think lovingly of you, *like a freshly pressed suit*
you are stepping into yourself
your empty shoes lie on the floor as if waiting for their
Santa Claus
Please come for me, I promise to be nice

XI

my poppa died
Goofo left for Hollywood

I went to Phipps in Baltimore
with my own white room and nurses round the clock
I wrote a novel in two months
and Rage! Goofo! Rage!
I can no longer dance nor paint nor write
you have nothing but rage

we live in a house named *La Paix*

we called the doctors in one day to hear our fight
and they wrote it down: 114 pages of our fury
and when the evening fell I knew you hated me
my Goofo, Do-Do, who the hell were you
the man I loved

when I read *Tender* it was indeed the end
they sent me to a place named Sheppard Pratt
and now I have two problems:
how to live and how to leave

there is nothing but despair
my only strength the Holy Book
I have to pray to live

XII

Now that there isn't any more happiness and
home is gone and there isn't even any past
and no emotions but those that were yours
I love you anyway,
even if there isn't any me or any love or any life

and somewhere in Hollywood
where you sent yourself postcards
just before Christmas your heart burst
Not even Scottie was surprised
nor the woman you were with
and I remembered you so well

it was a lovely dream we lived
when we were young

XIII

I am conversant with my position:
middle-aged, untrained, the graduate
of half a dozen homes for the insane
I walk correctly through a world I do not understand

where has my life gone to
beside the smell of paints and
the texture of the canvas in my rough and awkward hands?
a show of paper dolls and stories starring anguish
that's my artistic life

friends cared for Scottie and paid her way
she was ashamed of me I guess who wouldn't be?
a crazy mother then a grandmother
who sent her the occasional sketch

when I suffered asthma they sent me back to care
Don't worry Momma, I'm not afraid to die
but at night in a locked room what can one do
when the flames come licking at the doorknob
all the women screaming and no alarms or water

they knew it was me from the records of my teeth
one small charred slipper

XIV

remember the roses in Kenney's yard
you said "darling"
the wall was damp and mossy
when we crossed the street and said
we loved the south
you said you loved this lovely land
the wisteria along the fence was green
and the shade was cool and life was old

I am not buried there
yet my heart is in the South
where my magnolia still blooms and
Confederate jasmine perfumes the soft air

La Tendresse

Dora Carrington: March 29, 1893–March 11, 1932

I

today I saw a tattooed Venus

I spat upon my finger,
reached out to touch the canvas
with those mermaids, serpents,
sailors, tigers, vessels in full sail

the whorls of red and blue and black
like chapter headings in *Petite Larousse*
or my favourite paisley shawl

Venus turned indignantly

I forgot she was alive
she was that beautiful:
all agog in sea sights
and the sky

II

this is a love story:

I walked in the woods near Asheham,
the old man with a beard drew near

when he kissed me
I was appalled
no one believed me
it was both absurd and extreme

I crept into his bedroom at dawn
the intention was to sheer that beast
but when I leaned over
he opened his startling eyes
and I was hypnotized

I loved Lytton Strachey for all time

no matter he's a sodomite
and I a person of separate artistic degree
for sixteen years we loved each other with a tenderness
unparalleled

III

to be a girl is appalling

I have a slim and active frame
and that's what Lytton saw at first in me:
all wire and nerve,
the fascination of androgyny

Prussian eyes
a bell of wheaten hair

those cackling friends of his
they name me *baby face*
and mock my pointed toes
they call my eyes false innocent:

to them I am a heartless flirt
because the act disgusts me

IV

I saw my bottom first when I was five

I lay upon my nurse's lap
as she spanked my bare behind

I turned my head 'round:
oh how massive and how pink it was!

and worse, the monthly fiend that came upon me later
how the female body curses,
how it reeks and offends

V

my father was already old when I was born:
I loved to draw him as he sat at ease

Noel, Teddy, and me, we'd laugh so hard
I'd wet myself
but Mother and Lottie Louise
were nothing but furniture to me

here are the rules of my childhood:
do not speak about the body
wear your special clothes on Sunday
carry your prayer book in the open
whisper the word *confined*

I learned to be a liar,
left the provinces for London
and at the Slade won prizes for my drawings

like all good artists I'll be known forever
by only my last name

VI

I sketched my face at seventeen
lit up by flame at night:
thick strokes of lead,
a portrait without vanity,
blunt and looking back,
old beyond my years

to be pursued is terror and there's nothing but distaste

but I am drawn to the demeanour
and baroque ways of the rich
they like my homemade clothes
my dancing and always
my virginity

I love no one 'til I'm almost 23

and then the sumptuous paintings that I made:
the sonorous and layered oils,
Lytton with his Goya hands
pellucid eyes
Lady Strachey regal and half-blind
Annie in the kitchen

and our countryside:
rich as witchery and constant
a relief after a long and fearful span

VII

I fall in amongst the Bloomsberries:
they stroke me like a cat

but Lytton reads to me alone
as we lean by a cordial fire
and I bring him milky tea

to make a life of such tenderness!

a bower bird I'll be,
a sweet deep nest I'll wind
round his commodious limbs

but Lytton is a man in love with men
so a man I must draw near

my darling dream of three,
with Lytton loving Ralph who married me

VIII

we take delight in the meanderings, to Paris,
Venice, Yegen, and Madrid
and we talk and read and gossip while I paint
and make Lytton all my care

he is the centre and we moths
round his unrivalled flame

why do I feel no lust for Ralph
the way he urges me?
while he pricks another girl
his dear friend Gerald takes the lightning bolt for me
and I proceed to kiss and kiss him in the haystacks
on the hillsides on the beach
and practice lying to keep me safe and free

I never lied to Lytton
all his thoughts he shared with me

the complexity of this game
is enough to make me lose my aptitude for life:
should Ralph leave us, and the whole construction fall
there would be no point to breathing

IX

whilst I am busy with my brushes and my carving
a host of small commissions and
my orchard, garden, Millhouse still to keep,
Lytton grows to fame and is far courted
by gentry and the curious alike

I sit at home with puss and drink my whisky,
write the many letters and their frill
then hurry off to bed to listen to the rats

late at night the owl comes floating past my window,
in the dark I lie all nightmared and alone

Ralph loves Frances
but Lytton writes his love every day to me

I was never happy when I was without him
he was everything to me

X

Clive Bell said
there are no divorces in Bloomsbury,
only reshufflings:
Ralph lives with Frances
and though I sleep with Gerald, Henrietta, and Beakus
there is that incessant remorse

yet in the long and sweetest days with Lytton
we two are much at ease

I adored every hair, every curl of his beard,
devoured him as he read to me at night
loved the smell of his face on the sponge
the ivory skin on his hands, his voice
the sight of his hat as I watched it from my window
as it moved along behind the garden wall

XI

Lytton, the morning I knew you were dying
I lay in the closed garage with the chuggish motor running
but Ralph found me and made me live again

when I looked at your dead face it was so bleached and cold

I kissed your eyelids and your mouth
my tears dripped onto your fine face
I placed a crown of bay leaves on your head

and where did they take you?
I walked in the woods and felt nothing

please let me sit with your clothes in my arms
and smell you again and again
I want to hold your books and stand in your rooms alone
but they will not let me be

in the morning I saw Virginia who knows more than all the rest
she held me in her arms
the smell of her tobacco in the wool against my face

you will come and see us next week, or not, as you like, she said
I will come, or not, I said

XII

I waited two months before I took the rifle
and botched the very job:
I slowly bled to death upon the floor

I bade the doctor drink some sherry
he looked so beastly sad
when he tried to ease my pain

Ralph's stricken face forced yet another lie:
that I was shooting rabbits and I slipped

that's all, and died

they do not now remember where my ashes lie

love is love, and hard enough to find

Skinless

Carson McCullers: February 19, 1917–September 29, 1967

I

born in Georgia, I know the manners,
the shuffling and the Klan

my grandma I called Mommy
I slept with her and cozied in the dark,
she would say *Bring up the chair,*
darling, and climb to the top drawer of the bureau
There I would find some little goody:
cupcake or a kumquat, she was my first love

Mother told me I was favoured
tall at 14 and smoking with her on the back verandah
light pouring through the tangled blue and horror
of the South

we would hear that Mozart:
like God strutting in the night

II

I did not love my baby sister so one Christmas
I laid her out before the hearth
then showed my little brother
how Roman candles ricochet from wall to wall

flash fires in our hair and round our eyes,
shadows of the night outside

it took my jealousy away,
I laid the baby in the crib
and welcomed Santa Claus

Lamar was my father
my mother Marguerite
and I was Lula Carson Smith
until I grew too tall for that soft appellation

III

I will eat up anyone who'll let me
there is so much on earth I crave

I yearned for something, so
I sold Mommy's ring
and sailed for New York City,
crouched in phone booths reading books,
loved the interior life when I was seventeen

my body's the transgressor
or was it but the drink

my hand that shakes so hard I cannot hold a glass
my wrong feet in those shoes
I need somebody here to tie me in my clothes

the room fills up with heat
that same old gorgeous music on repeat

IV

I could have been a concert pianist
but my teacher left me for some less important life

the hours I'd spent at the piano
I turned to the page

read all of Mansfield, Proust, and the Russians,
always desired the snowy streets of Paris
flakes of ash and the grime of constant prowling,
my teeth were sharp those years,
Reeves was bright and dangerous
like a covert silk-sheathed knife

we are all one beneath our skins
there is no such thing as gender

V

Reeves stole my money so I left
and he made love with some sweet boy elsewhere

nights I'd wander Brooklyn like a jaunty little spook,
in a brainbox house Paul Bowles once watched me
teach a row of schoolgirls to conjugate the French
though the girls were *fictif*
and I'd knowledge *rien* of *français*, he loved me,
Janie loved me less and Wystan more,
and days I'd carve out words:
ten twenty thirty times a sentence
they'd flow like honey then I'd drink the bourbon straight
and we would talk and talk
offering our long smooth necks to notoriety

come here and kiss me,
whoever the hell you are

look deep into my face
then speak to me of all you see there
past a spirit flayed

VI

me and my foul mouth I must keep shut

I watch the way the wind moves in the trees
I recognize each leaf and bird
and I will think a long way off
so maybe I will go north and see snow
live in foreign lands

I come from a highway
of alcoholics
and married one but twice
I loved him so:
he looped the rope between us in the car
and said we could be hanging side by side

I fled to Paris for I was afraid
and Reeves came too, we lived on cognac
for a while until he found a hotel room
where he died, all my life I've been
too far from home

VII

can I turn myself outside in
and take the full impression of a human being?

I lay on the floor and begged an authoress
to let me worship,
she said she had some better time to waste
though I know I'm the finer writer of the two

and then the sea! and how to find the words
with whisky in the way and the sun,
I stood and guessed which man was which
and they would fall at my feet and marvel at my writing
self, my heart a lonely hunter even then

VIII

here's what liquor does:
it shows the hidden things
the undulations of the heart
whole sides of mountains crumbling loose
the yellow beak of day

rheumatic fever at 15,
a small explosion in the brain at 24,
I could not read nor tell the time
nor even walk:
I had to live it all again, my infancy

and this I understand:
the amber stain in a brandy snifter
the pungency of sherry tea
a plain and simple language of despair

IX

Give me a little drink
then I'll wander here and there and watch the sun
rise while the tang of grits and coffee
drifts out between the shade trees
and the infinite gradations of ghost

what I ponder is the fat man
so slender on the inside he could slip the needle's eye

imagine how life fatigues
how arduous to dream
when maybe one is hunchbacked
or staring transfixed at the lowly

X

I love to hug, I love to hug and hug
that's all

I imagine the ways it could be,
you and your astonishing faces:
I will beg to enter your bed
you will wrap me in your unfamiliar arms
and follow my rules of behaviour

the snow is falling on the river
the sweating glass
my walking stick abandoned

I am a mix of the delicious and curiosity,
my body but an envelope
all skeletal and reeking of smoke
and brandy wine,
I dress it in a negligee for meals

XI

so much time spent listening,
I'd turn and see some marvel in the shade,
some long-eyed freak appraising me
as if he knew my fate

but here I am: in bed
a leg raised up, no feeling in my side,
I wait for doctors' visits, their caring
sweet-breath'd words:
we will cut your leg off, sister,
and you'll be rich as Bernhardt

there is nothing like the South for aberration
though I lie here in my Hudson River'd view
and watch clouds wander round this room

Reeves dead, now Momma

I am so trepidacious
and fucking loud of need
don't shut me up now,
my tattered heart's fast filling up with snow

does anyone remember,
aside from faggots and the rags,
I wrote some perfect books when I was young

Complications Janie

Jane Auer Bowles: February 22, 1917–May 4, 1973

I

because I cannot recognize a colour
because I am no longer funny
do not mention a bird the desert brandy
all the stars at night
Cherifa's kisses
plates of couscous as we knelt close by the brazier
the way we had to bend our heads to pass

II

I'm a writer's writer's writer,
and what was writing but a misery to me?
the brawling over detail, syllable by spitting syllable
it's suicide

but here's my story:
my nurse dropped me as a baby and then my father died,
I fell again from horseback
but my leg did not heal fine: it was TB in the knee
so I spent two years tied up, in Switzerland

coming home I met Céline, the author, then I knew I was one too,
so wrote a novel lost somewhere and found my way
to all those Village bars,
no one knew me on my knees
in doorways, my mouth around a man
to find the cash to buy my girl
some food and proper clothes

no one thinks of ugly girls in bed:
their rustling, frightful eyeballs rolling in their heads,
I loved them because nobody else would

III

I'll talk about him one more time:
my father sat and died one night
when I was 13 and at camp where I love those beds
like one big family, row on row
I wish I had a dormitory everywhere
and I never mentioned him again

July night and all those people sleeping happy in a line:
Get into position, I'd say
and they would laugh and laugh

Do you love me?

I love an ugly girl

IV

naughty lovely at fifteen

while I was locked in traction,
I was tutored by a Frenchman versed in Greek mythology
and venereal disease
hell, what to do but study Proust, in infinite degree?

but when I'm home I've got a stiff knee and a limp
no one talks about the fact I'm Jewish
the aunts and Mother all lined up to see
how well I dress
and not to be mentioned in some circles
is the fact I plain love girls
and plain girls they are, too

men have no mystery: it's all on the outside
but women are profound,
mysterious, obscene

V

I fear sharks and elevators, mountains, dogs,
and being burned alive:
I'd like to know, who doesn't?

I cannot look down from a height
I cannot cross a bridge
but there's lots of fun in drinking,
my red and stand-up hair
a good long cozy cuddle
and me like Olive Oyl, my long and swinging arms
around your neck, my gamine smiles,
you think I'm lovely now
but I'll be homely later, filled with
sulks and tantrums, my little Chaplin limp
and broad sophistication: I am all of that

I spoke to a cop in Pittsburgh,
it was Christmas Eve and
I wore sandals in the snow:
Can you please direct me to the nearest cocktail center?
I mean right now, and this is what I need:
a long drink in my hand
a cigarette, a superbly shady bar

VI

I found a half man/woman
and we dated for a time, a night, once,
a while ago one evening
in the South

I cannot be contained, I want to be contained,
we must have said so many things, one to the other,
imagine darting of the tongues, confusion,
one last good look before I hopped the train
and made my true proposal: marry me, I said to Paul
though in truth *we're so incompatible*
we should live in a museum

he could play damn fine piano and
was cold as all I wanted in a man
and when he read my stories
he thought writing just the thing

I specialize in menus, line the parrot's cage with discord,
get involved in mischief, underscore the buzz

we want to travel here and there,
wild and full of charms
we are famous 'mongst the famous,
improbable amours
but I truly love my Bupple: he brings a suitcase full of ties
just anywhere

VII

in 1948 we came to Tangier
I thought I'd dreamt it, knew it so damn well

I walk the streets and touch the blue and chalky wash
upon the walls and houses, I cannot slake my longing
for the town

Once I reached to touch a beautiful and powdered clown
because I felt such yearning
it was at a little circus
but I was not a child

in the market I saw Cherifa: *she's that kind,*
completely beautiful, a little smaller than myself,
strong shoulders, legs with lots of hair
skin soft and soft
We went up onto the topmost terrace, looked at all Tangier:
the boats and stars, the line of lights along the beach,
the wind was cold, Cherifa shivered,
I kissed her just a little,
Had God seen us? she enquired

VIII

I wrote a book, *Two Serious Ladies*
they said in print I was the best, they cooed it to my face:
Williams, Burroughs, and Capote
all of the above

good writing is like guilt
but I cannot find that way again
so cook and serve and drink and make them laugh

my hands are strange and busy
like a man's
they're soft and boneless
and when you touch them they just let you in

I eat my pills like candy
and I wash them down with drink:
a big big bowl of goodies near the sink

Cherifa is a witch, they say,
I do what she tells me for she has such rage
and Paul says love is lying, it's a schizophrenic break
his parents never loved him like my mother did

IX

I live on tiptoe, gulping alcohol and angst
and what I love the most is daily life
amidst the liars of the souk: the clever pouring of the tea,
the dusty green of cumin, wild artichoke, and fennel,
whispers, bowls of scarlet powder, a kiss upon the cheek,
caliginous magic, my wallet open on the floor:
Cherifa's eyes that wander here and here

Paul can travel all he wants,
write and try to hide from fame
but I will stay and manage my sweet harem

what's the use of a brain if it's not used?
the howl of desert wind like some huge and pointless fire

I stare at my writing materials as though they were Nazis
and Cherifa slouches there like Marlon Brando,
all cigarette and camp

X

am I their fag hag or do pansies love me best?
Paul's boys, plus Ginsberg, Auden, and the rest:
let's tell the truth now: Crippie Kike Dyke, that's me!
I make them laugh like crazy, bring Paul tea and burger
on a tray, on time, each night:
I know a wifely thing or two and he and I
we'll sit and talk disaster,
we enjoy that just the most
and a good cry here and there for the fun of it

my mind, Paul says, is an invention by Kafka
and he is proud and sad to leave me lonely on the sand dunes

then I turn forty and I have my stroke

when the inside is dying there can be a new joy
a joy so false one is shaken with mirth
when the joy is true
and the inside alive
one can never feel the same

XI

dear Mrs Bowles you are not coping
go back to your pots and pans and cope

phenobarbs like strolling in a smokestack sniffing clouds
sepasil epanutin mellaril a lovely sounding thing
my teeth grind on and brandy does the swish
with valium seconal and other little pills
like Smarties down my throat

forget my name and get a wig
do hair tricks for strangers just to get a laugh
hang my clothes upon my bones and have a fight
drinking all the way to *amusant* and seizure

Mommie comes to see me: I can no longer hide
the fact I'm going mad:
my future is the loony bin
and blindness leads the way

XII

one novel, one play, a few short stories:
my legacy of publication
yet they call me famous and beyond compare

I do not know no more
for I embrace the crucifix
a small white bed in Málaga my home
sweet Sisters tend me there

Paul marked my grave with nothing
just the flotsam of a Spanish windy day
he turned away
unhappy man
and surely nothing more to say

Ardent

Elizabeth Smart: December 27, 1913–March 4, 1986

I

life is murder
and art is even worse:
do I dare to plunge into this journey?

put on the clarinet quintet in A,
let Mozart help me through

I find as many answers there
as anywhere

a happy little pill unwinds me

II

what I remember best is Kingsmere,
my truest paradise:
I recognize each rock and root,
the path unwinding to the boathouse,
the leap of leopard frogs against the still midday,
the dark cool water of the lake

storms roil beyond the waving mapled hills
and up through pines to where I crouch (the creaking lovely floor)
to clip my fashioned paper dolls and
memorize the genus of each blessed simple thing:
implicit ferns unfolding in the shade,
mouths of giant pike, their googly eyes,
the mountain, its mantle-sweetened air

nighttime: the humped raccoons beyond the walls
creep past my torpid bedstead,
the empty sighing lounge chairs,
stains of misplaced highballs,
feather ticking, dawn

III

in the fall, back to Ottawa for the Smarts,
the chill air on Beechwood, green stiff skirts of
uniforms, my sisters and I walking
through the darkened Elmwood doors,
good girls, all of us

I loved to see the youngest ones at play
in the wooden toy house near Springfield, the door so small
you'd wonder how a baby could pass through, perfect housewives
practicing

the sound of Mummy's wails at night in winter,
the sight of her adrift in snow,
or pacing on the balcony or rolling round the bathroom floor,
my sister Helen's dress torn off, her tender breasts exposed,
face slapped and baby Russel crying,
a small body sobbing in a bed of maple leaves

Daddy read his lawyer's letters and laid truth down like matting:
this is how we lived and we were lonely

IV

my god the hell of Ottawa!
there's never been a place so dismal:
bloody invitations to the *après* ski,
an afternoon of skating up at Rideau Hall,
the Little Theatre evenings

then London, where Jane and I were sovereigns,
I'd forage every alley for something crammed with meaning,
anything relentless, captivating, whole,
I knew one day I'd find it
knew it in my bones, my sex

we lived the life that Mummy never did,
and when she came to town her balm would sweep us in:
her lovely smell, her underwear, her shopping sprees,
she was warm extravagant delicious

and then she'd turn to me and say *I've hated you all day,*
you're the meanest little thing,
any child could write this drivel

I must marry a poet
it's the only thing

V

all these summers Kingsmere,
a private lovely life with leaves and earth,
wild geese and Dutchman's breeches,
hepaticas and blood root,
bird song, the smell of mornings after rain,
pleasing mother, being self: my body but a seam
that rips from end to end

huge diversions of the upper class:
dress-up parties at the King Estate,
dancing on our screened verandahs,
my journals overflow with incantation,
bucking back the emptiness with language

one day in Better Books in Charing Cross
I found the poems of a man named Barker
and told the world that I would marry him

this is what I want: art, love, and children:
do not stoop to offer less than everything

VI

waiting for the bus in Monterey
I changed my lipstick often
and considered what the future held:
his wife climbed down, so thin and shy
so dark against my shining head

I must be radiant, aglow, on fire:
we drive to where we live, nearby, in huts

George Barker's hand on mine
his arm against my nipple
the whole world rocking
I try so hard to be polite
until he comes upon me in the water

and now I love the night, the legs of children, tall poinsettia, hydrangeas
and the lemon trees, I love the residential palms that dress in pantaloons,
I love the birds in pepper trees, the sun on swimming pools

the multitude of kisses, never enough skin to sate me
it is no surprise I am arrested at the Arizona border
because he is my love and I am his,
who cares for his English class awareness, prissy wife:
can there be life or breath apart from this?

in the mornings I am ill with child at Pender Harbour,
I write my book, desire made flesh and rhetoric:
By Grand Central Station I Sat Down and Wept
was birthed two weeks before Georgina

I do not mind my child a bastard:
it will help them to avoid the bores, the snobs,
the petty, the afraid

VII

I had four in total,
my darlings, all my dreams

we lived with nothing yet I smocked their clothes,
made nettle soup, held honeyed bodies in my arms,
bleached nappies in the dark, wiped noses, rode them here
and there upon my bike, smoked and drank and wept
and George would come and leave his seed behind,
but never any cash or caring, just an Ottawa allowance
and I lived so far away, in farms in England or wherever
costs were few: a low wet cottage in the Irish hills,
bedsits in London, barnyards, attics

oh beloved friends, oh stagger me with cases
bottles clunking well into the weekend drunk

George, I beg you, *I am so afraid,*
of wind, the empty house, the air raids, burglars
lunatics and ghouls, catastrophe, appearances and
death. You must do something
for I am simply going mad

you are my husband and my one true love
no matter how many other wives
post you their midnight dreams

VIII

Georgina, Christopher, Sebastian, and then Rose:
the womb's an unwieldy baggage.
Who can stagger uphill with such a noisy weight?

To send the children to good schools
with clean and decent clothing, lots of books,
I worked *Queen*, worked *Vogue*,
I was the best copywriter in the city
sat at desk sniffed glue held phone typed hard took drink
wrote fast and funny, hard and real,
scurried through the filthy streets harassed by deadlines,
took pills, the crystal clear dependency: bloody sharp, that focus,
I ground my teeth

put my feet up on the weekends, wellies on the workbench,
dead soldiers piling up below

what is left of my youth rushes up like a geyser
as I sit in the sun combing lice from my hair

IX

how to survive life's script?
you pray and bang your head,
be beautiful, wait, love, rage, rail;
look and possibly, if lucky, see;
love again; try to stop loving,
go on loving, bustle about, rush to and fro;
whatever you say will be far less than truth

I saw my children off to life
and turned alone back down the bitter lane,
BBC sonatas in the kitchen, empty page,
I am *desperate from hating*
pushed too far to do too much

but then the strangest thing:
my little book revived and I am famous!
the heady stuff of praise and recognition
sets me restless and all atremble

there is money and I fix a place to live
and work a garden there,
crawl on my hands and knees upstairs to bed,
why not? tricks, sleight of hand, anything it takes

and in the mornings I rise and toil
amidst the pits and rumblings of the earth:
how dear it is to birth a flower,
hold a cutting, name a thing
and they wind quite round about me
like my children always did

I begin a poem here and there
small things, aflutter more than most
then Rose takes up the needle
so I hold her children too

X

Death By Misadventure,
so they said, we buried Rose

when one's own heart-child goes to death
what's left?
nothing wards
no language

why did I not tell her what I knew:
the long bitterness of life
the mean, the ungenerous
the need to forge capacities for pain

George has many children
what's one less, the one he laid his hands on
seldom, gone for good

life is *the roll of matter heaving into heaven*
in its painful individual way

xi

they asked me back to Canada
to talk about the craft
I drank away the bleak lot where I lived
friends turned their heads in fear and bald disgust
the late night coffee shops and men
the vomit on the rugs

then home at last
clematis everywhere and rain
worm was my best beast friend
mud was my first love

I adore this twisted acre
and lie in bed remembering
calling out in sleep for Mummy
what these nightmares bring me to I dread

when these pills kick in I open up my head to memory
and fear, whole notebooks filling late at night
with writing near impossible to read
but it is there, you find it if you can
make from it all whatever books you wish

Acknowledgements

The following materials were essential in my research: *On Iniquity*, by Pamela Handsford Johnson; *The Sisters*, by Mary S. Lovell; *Diana Mosley*, by Jan Dalley; *Unity Mitford: A Quest*, by David Pryce-Jones; *Save Me The Waltz*, by Zelda Fitzgerald; *Zelda Fitzgerald: Her Voice in Paradise*, by Sally Cline; *Tender Is the Night*, by F. Scott Fitzgerald; *Carrington*, by Gretchen Gerzina; *Chrome Yellow*, by Aldous Huxley; *The Art of Dora Carrington*, by Jane Hill; *Carrington: Letters and Extracts from her Diaries*, chosen by David Garnett; *The Lonely Hunter*, Virginia Spencer Carr; *The Collected Works of Carson McCullers*; *The Complete Stories of Truman Capote*; *A Little Original Sin*, by Millicent Dillon; *The Dream at the End of the World*, by Michelle Green; *My Sister's Hand in Mine*, by Jane Bowles; *Women of the Beat Generation*, by Brenda Knight; *Minor Characters*, by Joyce Johnson; *Let It Come Down: The Life of Paul Bowles* (film) by Jennifer Baichwal; *By Heart: The Life of Elizabeth Smart*, by Rosemary Sullivan; *By Grand Central Station I Sat Down and Wept*, by Elizabeth Smart; *Autobiographies*, by Elizabeth Smart; *Elizabeth's Garden*, by Elizabeth Smart; *Necessary Secrets*, by Elizabeth Smart. Direct quotations taken from these sources are italicized.

Thank you to the Canada Council for the Arts, the Ontario Arts Council's Work-in-Progress and Writers' Reserve granting programs, and to the Queen's University Fund for Scholarly Research & Creative Work.

I am grateful to the following for their ongoing critiques and fellowship: Jill Battson, Susan Glickman, Genni Gunn, Robert McGill, Moez Surani, and John Emil Vincent.

The commentary and suggestions from Ingrid de Kok and Jan Conn were invaluable.

Thank you to Sarindar Dhaliwal for allowing the use of her image on the cover of this book. It is taken from her painting *Interior/Exterior Zanzibar Tea Gardens*.

Maureen Scott Harris and Kitty McKay Lewis have encouraged and befriended me for years. Barry Dempster supported this manuscript right from the start. Elizabeth Phillips offered the toughest, truest criticism and fine-tuned editing I could possibly imagine.

As always, Kenneth: my love and gratitude.

C arolyn Smart is the author of four previous volumes of poetry, including *Stoning the Moon* and *The Way to Come Home*. An excerpt from her memoir *At the End of the Day* won first prize in the CBC Literary Contest (Personal Essay Category) in 1993. She is the founder of the Bronwen Wallace Award for Emerging Writers, and since 1989 has taught Creative Writing at Queen's University. Since 1983 she has lived in the country north of Kingston with her husband and sons.